FREDA & JEM'S BEST OF THE WEEK

by Lois Fine

PLAYWRIGHTS CANADA PRESS
Toronto

Freda & Jem's Best of the Week © 2016 by Lois Fine

For professional or amateur production rights, please contact:
The Playwrights Guild of Canada
401 Richmond Street West, Suite 350
Toronto, ON M5V 3A8
416-703-0201, orders@playwrightsguild.ca

LIBRARY AND ARCHIVES CANADA CATALOGUING IN PUBLICATION
Fine, Lois, author
    Freda & Jem's best of the week / Lois Fine.

A play.
Issued in print and electronic formats.
ISBN 978-1-77091-507-7 (paperback).–ISBN 978-1-77091-508-4 (pdf).–
ISBN 978-1-77091-509-1 (html).–ISBN 978-1-77091-510-7 (mobi)

    I. Title. II. Title: Freda and Jem's best of the week.

PS8611.I54F74 2016   C812'.6   C2016-900211-X
                                                    C2016-900212-8

We acknowledge the financial support of the Canada Council for the Arts, the Ontario Arts Council (OAC), the Ontario Media Development Corporation, and the Government of Canada through the Canada Book Fund for our publishing activities. Nous remercions l'appui financier du Conseil des Arts du Canada, le Conseil des Arts de l'Ontario (CAO), la Société de développement de l'industrie des médias de l'Ontario, et le Gouvernement du Canada par l'entremise du Fonds du livre du Canada pour nos activités d'édition.

 Canada Council Conseil des arts
for the Arts du Canada

 ONTARIO ARTS COUNCIL
CONSEIL DES ARTS DE L'ONTARIO
an Ontario government agency
un organisme du gouvernement de l'Ontario

  Ontario
Ontario Media Development
Corporation

Freda & Jem's Best of the Week was first produced by Buddies in Bad Times Theatre in Toronto from September 13 to October 5, 2014. It featured the following cast and creative team:

Freda: Diane Flacks
Jem: Kathryn Haggis
Sam: Sadie Epstein-Fine
Teejay: Stephen Joffe

Directed by Judith Thompson
Live music by Lorraine Segato
Set and costume design by Camellia Koo
Lighting design by Kimberly Purtell
Stage management by Sharon DiGenova

CHARACTERS

Freda: forty-eight, fem lesbian
Jem: forty-seven, butch lesbian
Sam: seventeen, Freda and Jem's daughter
Teejay: fourteen, Freda and Jem's son

SCENE 1.

JEM   I am a butch dyke. Think about it like this—I'm not a girl, I'm a boy. I'm not a man, I'm a woman. Us butches, we recognize each other on the street, but we don't say anything. That would be like breaking the butch code. But there's something—it's in the eyes—a look that passes between us, and we wonder in that moment about each other. What happened to you? Did you find someone to love you? Did you let her touch you deep down inside? Did you manage to hang on to her? Or did she leave you in the dust with her name on your tongue?

SCENE 2.

Music as FREDA, SAM, *and* TEEJAY *enter. Even though no words are spoken, it is clear that* SAM *and* TEEJAY *are being told that their moms are breaking up.*

SCENE 3.

Flashback scene to FREDA *and* JEM'*s first meeting. In a dyke bar. On the crowded dance floor.*

FREDA   Oops—sorry.

JEM   Don't be.

FREDA   It's so crowded, I—

JEM   Don't worry about it, I would have asked you anyways—

Pause.

To dance.

FREDA   Really—

JEM   I saw you—

FREDA   You did—

JEM   Yeah, those moves—

JEM imitates FREDA's dancing.

FREDA dances away, then comes back.

What's your name?

FREDA   Freda.

JEM   Does that mean you're free?

FREDA   I might be—

JEM   How about free and easy?

FREDA   I might be that too—define "easy."

JEM   There's easygoing.

FREDA   Not really.

JEM   There's easy to talk to.

FREDA   That's probably true.

JEM   There's easy on the eyes—no, don't answer that, that's a given.

FREDA   Awww . . . that's sweet—a bit of a sleazy pickup line but I'll let it go. This time.

JEM   There's easy over.

FREDA   What??

JEM   Like eggs the morning after.

FREDA   The morning after. Right. I unh—

JEM   Well, Freda, free and easy—thank you for the dance.

FREDA   Wait. What about you?

JEM   What—

FREDA   Aren't you going to tell me your name?

JEM   My name's Jem.

FREDA   Jem.

JEM   Not like the diamond.

FREDA   No?

JEM   More like the diamond in the rough.

FREDA   I see. Well, good to meet you, Jem.

JEM   Good to meet you too.

FREDA   We haven't exactly met.

JEM   I like the sound of your voice.

FREDA	Oh yeah?
JEM	And the way you talk, the way your eyebrows go up and down—has anyone ever told you that before, about your eyebrows? It's cute. I like it.
FREDA	Do you say this to everyone you meet on this dance floor? Wait, don't answer that—you'll spoil my fantasy.
JEM	You're having a fantasy? About me?
FREDA	You're funny—and you're a good talker.
JEM	I'm the whole package—
FREDA	Un-hunh.
JEM	Seriously, I'm deeper than you think.
FREDA	Okay . . .
JEM	And I'm a plumber—I understand pipes and water and flow.
FREDA	Flow—I like flow.
JEM	And flush? Like the way you look right now—

They slow dance. It's electric. First kiss.

SCENE 4.

JEM   I'm fifteen, and me and my best friend—Dana—we go to her house after school, into her room, and we close the door. And I tickle her back. I start off in slow, concentric circles, hypnotizing her almost, and she kind of sighs, like "haaaaaaaaa." It starts over her shirt. And then one day I go under her shirt. And then . . . one day . . . we get the idea that she should take her shirt off. And I tickle her back, along her bra, down her sides, and when I get to her sides she raises herself up a bit—you know, so I can get under—and then I tickle her from underneath—so gently. I am holding my breath—she's lifting up even more, sighing.

I take a deep breath—I pray I am giving her exactly what she wants. I close my eyes and I touch her breasts—she doesn't move away. I go lower, between her legs. I feel something. It's—wet? I mean, I didn't know about wet. I mean, I am touching her in places I have never even touched on me.

When it's over—when she decides that it's enough, her signal is to squirm in a certain way—I ever so slowly, imperceptibly move into a sitting position and kind of look away for a moment while she puts her clothes back on. And then we turn on the TV, never speaking about it, knowing that we will do it again the next day.

SCENE 5.

Present. Kitchen.

FREDA I don't need your guilt trips, Jem—if you don't want to stay home just say so. Fine, I won't go out then. I don't need your whiney little attitude.

JEM My whiney little attitude?

FREDA Yes, Jem, that's what I said.

JEM Well guess what—I don't think you're going out to any Queer Censorship anything. I think you're going out somewhere else.

FREDA Right. And why do you have to say it like that? Why do you have to make fun of it?

JEM Queers Against Censorship—as in QUAC—come on, lighten up, Freda. Besides, you're the one who's rubbed my nose in it for the past two years, like suddenly everyone has to be "queer," like saying butch is a bad word.

FREDA   You have to admit, you are stuck in a little bubble, but I guess that's not my problem anymore.

JEM   What's that supposed to mean—

FREDA   Just a hint, Jem—when you get out there, you might find the scene has changed in twenty-one years, that's all. You might want to say "queer" instead of "dyke" and maybe try "gender queer" instead of "butch."

JEM   Thanks for the tip—glad I've been paying for your fancy education.

FREDA   Look, Jem, we have *three* more weeks to get through. You're out of here in three weeks and you can't be civil to me—

JEM   What? You're the one—

FREDA   There you go, Jem, be defensive. Are you that allergic to new ideas?

JEM   When they come with that snotty little attitude, yes I am.

FREDA   Why do I bother?

JEM   You're seeing someone else.

FREDA   *I'm not.*

JEM   BULLSHIT. WHO IS IT?

Silence from FREDA.

TELL ME WHO.

FREDA   *Nobody—stop it.*

SAM *and* TEEJAY *enter.*

SAM   Stop what?

TEEJ   So, Moms, I'm starving—when's dinner?

SAM   I thought you said no fighting for these three
weeks?

FREDA   Teejay, can you not leave your bag on the stairs . . .
and you know what, Sam, you're seventeen years
old, *you* can make dinner.

SAM   What? Why are you being so rude to *me?* What
did I do?

JEM   Tell me about it.

FREDA   Don't do that, Jem—stay out of it. This is between
me and the kids.

TEEJ   No. Stop *fighting.*

JEM	Your kids—they're *my* kids too, okay?
FREDA	I never said *my* kids. I said *the* kids.
SAM	*Fuck* this!
JEM	All the time—*your* kids.
SAM	*(to JEM) Mom, stop it—*
TEEJ	Moms, I'm starving—you said spaghetti tonight—
FREDA	*Jem.* For god's sake. Can you just give it up? Yes, they are your kids. Did I ever say they weren't? I have *never* made them into *my* kids—you're the one who raises it.
JEM	Oh, great, let it all out, Freda.
SAM	You're being horrible.
TEEJ	*You're* being horrible, Sam.
SAM	*Right,* Teejay, and you're not? Fine. Assholes!

SAM exits.

FREDA	Sam—
TEEJ	Fine. I'll eat at Brian's if there's no dinner here.

TEEJ exits.

FREDA   What? *Teejay*—

JEM   Freda, we can't do this—they *need* us.

FREDA   They don't need us like this, Jem—

JEM   Can't we try one more time, Freda. We can fix this.

FREDA   We can't.

JEM   We have to.

FREDA   Jem, we've been through it a hundred times.

JEM   We haven't.

FREDA   We have. We've made our decision.

JEM   There *is* someone else. Look me in the eye and tell me there isn't.

SCENE 6.

TEEJ   *I hate apartments.* I don't want to live in two places. How will I remember *two* postal codes? I already put my address down on like a hundred school forms. What am I supposed to do, *erase* them? I'll never find any of my stuff—I'll be late for school every day. They can't force me. I'll go to Brian's. I'm not going to some stupid new apartment.

SAM   They are both so full of shit. They make it seem like it's all going to be so fine and easy. Jem will get an apartment and you'll each get your own new room—with a *bay window*—the perfect lesbian divorce. *Fucking lies!*

TEEJ   I should have *known* this—it was so obvious—they never eat dinner at the same time, one of them is always out. They don't watch TV together anymore—they used to *love* that. At night we could always hear them whispering in their bed—they sounded so happy.

SAM   All I wanted to do was come home and talk to them today. All this shit I'm going through, I just needed to come *home*.

TEEJ   I hear talking—more like hissing—ugly sounds like cats make when they're backed up against a wall with no way out.

SCENE 7.

Flashback. JEM *is unpacking a box.*
FREDA *walks in with a box. They have
just moved in.*

FREDA   Butch prep school, eh?

JEM   You've never heard of butch prep school, woman?
I'm sure you've had other lovers graduate from
it. Come on, every dyke knows about it. It's where
butches learn all the rules—three years of regular
schooling and fourth year honour code.

FREDA   Butch honour code—is that where you slay the
dragon and lay your jacket across a puddle so the
little lady can walk across—

JEM   *Hey!* Not funny. Honour code year means a lot to us.

FREDA   Okay, so what'd you learn? Like give me an
example.

JEM Well, there's all the basic stuff, like Butch Training
101—you know, holding open doors, which by the
way is not as easy as it looks. Oh yeah, and there's
a long course on listening—they teach you the
facial moves, the eye contact, the slow nod. There's
how to swagger. There's soft butch classes and
hard butch classes—like, can you be a butch if you
don't have a pocket for your socket, or can you still
maintain your butch integrity if you scream when a
mouse runs out from under your barbecue cover?

FREDA Did they teach you to talk in that low, sexy voice to
drive all the women wild?

JEM No.

FREDA You know, sometimes I call the answering machine
just to hear you say "hello."

JEM Get out—okay—last box.

> *JEM unpacks her grandmother's
> candlesticks.*

FREDA Hey, what are those? What, can't I see them? Are
they a present from an ex or something?

JEM They're from my grandmother.

FREDA Wow, they're beautiful. Hey, let's do it. I've always
wanted to—the whole Shabbat thing. I'm not
religious or anything, but the ritual—so ancient—
it's like we get to pause every Friday night, catch

our breath, and light these candles from your grandmother . . . at our new kitchen table. You and me—

JEM   Every Friday night. Wow . . .

FREDA   I was just saying we could try it.

JEM   No, no, it's just that— No one has ever wanted to be with me—like this—before.

FREDA   Hey, I'm not going anywhere.

They kiss.

SCENE 8.

JEM   I had a low voice as a kid. Really low. Too low—for a
girl. I'm six years old when I answer the phone one
day and some guy says to me, "What's your name,
little boy?" I hang up and tell my parents. My dad
says, "That's it," and they take me to the Montreal
Children's Hospital—Voice Pathology. My father says,
"Fix it." The doctor is pretty and she shows me how
to do voice exercises to make my voice sound higher.

Every day I sit in front of the mirror with my earlobes turned inside out, my neck raised up, and in
the highest voice I can find, I repeated what the
doctor told me to say: "Sweet meat, neat seat, eat
feet, sweet meat." I am so diligent about doing my
voice exercises. The kids on my block would ask if
I can come out to play but my parents say, "She's
busy." The kids must have spied on me because
when I finally go out to play they are all standing
there with their hands on their earlobes, their ears
turned inside out, and they are all saying:

SAM &
TEEJ   "Sweet meat, neat seat, eat feet, sweet meat."

SCENE 9.

Present. SAM *and* FREDA *are talking in*
FREDA*'s bed.*

SAM   Don't you think you should have made sure you
        really loved each other before you had kids? Just
        saying.

FREDA   It's not that simple. You think it's going to last
        forever.

SAM   I'd make sure. Not that I'm ever going to have a
        relationship.

FREDA   Don't say that—you'll have great relationships.

SAM   Look where it got you.

FREDA   It got us you, and Teejay.

SAM   Then stay together. What about how she makes you
        laugh. You know, her special way. She's the only one

who can do that. Mom, she loves you so much. And you love her. Why are you doing this?

FREDA   We have no choice, Sam.

SAM   Why?

FREDA   We fight all the time.

SAM   So?

FREDA   You like living in a house where your parents fight all the time?

SAM   It's better than breaking up. Why are you *doing* this? Think about us. What about Teejay? Do you ever think of him? He's a mess.

FREDA   He is not—he's fine.

SAM   He is not fine, but how would you know, you're never home anymore—

FREDA   That's not true. I'm home all the time. I went out two nights this week. You think I *ever* wanted to hurt you? Or Teejay? You both are my life.

SAM   *Ohh*, are you going to *cry* now? I hope you *feel* like a bad mother. Because you *are*.

FREDA   Sam!

SAM	Ruin our lives forever and it's *fine.* You think I'm so fine, so together. *I'm not—*
FREDA	I know that.
SAM	*No you don't, or you wouldn't do this? How could you do this? I hate you!*
FREDA	I'm sorry—

> *It takes them a long time to put them-*
> *selves back together but eventually* FREDA
> *is able to comfort* SAM.

SAM	She's gonna get a new girlfriend, you know.
FREDA	Eventually, I guess she might.
SAM	I'm gonna hate her.
FREDA	You can hate her for a while.
SAM	I'm gonna hate her forever. And yours too. Wait, do you already have one?

> *Silence from* FREDA.

> *You coward!!*

> SAM *exits.*

SCENE 10.

TEEJ They keep trying to teach me how the washing machine works. They want me to do my own laundry but I like it better when they do it. But I've been thinking, you know, what if I did learn—separate the whites and all the colours, throw in a capful of detergent, make sure it's a cold wash, then Jem wouldn't have to do it when she gets home from work tired, and Freda won't have to defend me and make excuses for me. They wouldn't fight about it. That's it, starting right now I'm doing the laundry.

SCENE 11.

Flashback. At the dinner table. The
Shabbat candles are lit.

FREDA   Okay, best of the week.

JEM   Let's see. I guess I have to say my best of the week is
this moment—right here with all of you.

SAM   Mom, that's what you say all the time.

JEM   That's cuz it's true, sweetheart. Twelve years later
and this is still the best place in the whole world
for me.

TEEJ   Well my best of the week was acing the math quiz
and getting rocky road ice cream. Hey, Mom, can
we watch a movie tonight?

JEM   Hold on, hold on, let's go around. Sam's turn.

SAM	My best of the week was when I got my Bronze Cross. Oh ya, oh ya.
FREDA	Do you know how proud we are of you, honey?
SAM	I know—deep water spinals, hardest thing ever.
JEM	You were awesome.
SAM	Thanks.
JEM	What about you, babe? What's your best of the week?
FREDA	I'm with you, Jem. This is a pretty good moment.
SAM	Boring, Mom. Come on, get creative.
TEEJ	Yeah, every week, same old thing—this moment with you kids. "Kids, this is the only place I want to be right now" over and over. Make up something good.
FREDA	What would I say? I could make something up.
JEM	You could guess. We could both guess—that would be two guesses—or would that be a "guess-i." Get it—guess-I?
SAM	Mom, you're so crazy.
JEM	Not as crazy as you.

TEEJ   What about as crazy as me?

JEM   Not as crazy as you either.

FREDA   Well, I'm crazy too.

JEM   Well, I'm crazy *about* all of you. We're all crazy!

SCENE 12.

FREDA   When they were little we would put them in their pyjamas and take them out to the drive-in—the first movie for them and the second one for us. We'd drive home with them sleeping in the back of the car and Jem would say, "Does everyone have it this good or is it just us?" And I would say, "It's just us," and then the kids learned to say that too—"Does everyone have it this good?"

SAM,
TEEJ,
& FREDA   "It's just us."

FREDA   And they would just love that. We promised we would love them to the moon. That doesn't include telling them that they are going to live in two places and that their moms are better as friends and then watching them dissolve in front of our eyes. Yesterday I was walking through a street fair and I saw this angel—carved right out of a tree—it's hard, wooden wings—and I thought, "I will protect you. You *will* be *fine.*"

SCENE 13.

Present. Kitchen. JEM *and* TEEJ *doing homework.*

JEM   Come on, bud—you asked me to help you, pay attention here.

TEEJ   Hey, Mom, you know how you're always saying I should tell you what's on my mind?

JEM   Yeah?

TEEJ   And that I shouldn't feel embarrassed?

JEM   Yeah?

TEEJ   Even if it's guy stuff?

JEM   That's right, buddy—you can talk to me.

TEEJ   Brian's brother Eddy says that the Beatles song—the one where they go, "Happiness is a warm gun"—do you know that song? Eddy says it's about a wet dream.

JEM   Eddy says that, does he?

TEEJ   Is it true? Is that what the song's about?

JEM   I don't know. What do you think?

TEEJ   I believe Eddy.

JEM   Oh yeah? What else does Eddy tell you?

TEEJ   Oh, lots of things, like how usually shy girls like guys who talk a lot and girls who talk a lot like shy guys.

JEM   Wow. Eddy teaches you guys some really good stuff. *So*, you a shy guy or a gabby guy?

TEEJ   Shy guy probably.

JEM   Well, let's make you into a math guy—come on, back to the books, eh?

TEEJ   Aw, do I have to?

JEM   Yeah, you do. But hey, bud—thanks for telling me that, what you just did. I didn't realize that was happening to you, that wet dream stuff—

TEEJ   *Mom! That's disgusting! I wasn't talking about me! Ewww.*

JEM	I thought you said—
TEEJ	Forget it—you don't understand anything. It's like how Eddy always wants to talk about girls and sex and he's like, "You guys can talk to me, don't worry, brothers' code of honour," but then Brian goes, "We don't like anyone yet; we just like our video games." I don't know why people don't get it. I mean, I might get a girlfriend some day—I mean I've thought about it—but for now, all I really care about is my high score, you know?
JEM	High score. Okay. And here I thought you were trying to tell me something else. You know, about yourself.
TEEJ	*Mom!!*
JEM	All right, never mind, change the subject. Here we go—math. Two more, come on—
TEEJ	I said I don't want to.
JEM	Teejay . . .
TEEJ	*Quit yelling at me!!!*
JEM	I'm not yelling, for god's sake, Teejay—I am talking.
TEEJ	*No you're not. You're yelling. You always yell.*
JEM	Whoa, whoa, Teejay—

TEEJ   *That's why we're breaking up.*

JEM   That's not true. *Stop it, Teejay!*

TEEJ   *See, you are yelling—*

JEM   *Goddamn you, Teejay.*

TEEJ   *Don't swear at me.*

      FREDA enters.

FREDA   Jem, what is going on??

TEEJ   *She keeps yelling at me. I told her to stop but she doesn't.*

JEM   This is nuts. I wasn't yelling, for *chrissakes.*

FREDA   Jem, if Teejay says you were yelling, then I believe him. Why are you getting him so upset?

TEEJ   *I hate this house.*

JEM   I'm getting him upset? I'm getting *him upset?* You know what? I don't give a damn. *You're all full of shit!*

      JEM exits.

FREDA   Great, Jem, walk out. Here we go, someone says the littlest thing and *you walk out*—you can dish it out but *you can't take it.*

TEEJ   She hates me—

FREDA	She doesn't hate *you*, sweetheart.
TEEJ	I'm calling my dad.
FREDA	You can call him but he's not your dad.
TEEJ	He said I could call him Dad.
FREDA	He is *Brian's* dad, Teejay. *Steven* is *Brian's* dad.
TEEJ	I said, "I don't think my moms would like that," and he said, "Well, surely even *they* must know that every fellow needs a father."
FREDA	Really!
TEEJ	I've already started calling him Dad anyways.
FREDA	You have?
TEEJ	Yes I have—and I like it.
FREDA	Great, go for it—
TEEJ	What's the big deal if I want to call him Dad anyways, it's not hurting anyone.
FREDA	Right. You're right—
TEEJ	Why are you going so crazy?
FREDA	I am not going crazy—I am being perfectly calm.

TEEJ Yes, that *is* how you go crazy—

FREDA You want Steven to be your dad? Really? Of all
the great men in your life you are choosing
Steven. Why?

TEEJ I like him.

FREDA He hardly speaks—every time I see him the most he
does is nod—like as if a nod is a word.

TEEJ Mom, that's just a guy thing—you don't understand.

FREDA Fine, see what it's like to have Steven as your dad. I
really don't care.

TEEJ Why are you yelling at me?

FREDA I am not yelling, Teejay. I am talking.

TEEJ I thought we reinvent families.

FREDA Yes we do, but we don't just give ourselves a father.
Steven is not your father, Teejay. Does Steven sit up
with you and help you with your homework? No, he
does not. Does Steven take you for new shoes? No,
Jem does that. Does Steven cook you dinner? Does
he even know that beets give you a rash? Does he
know you don't like goat cheese? Did Steven teach
you to wash your hair the pain-free method that Jem
invented? Did he wake up at five in the morning for
three years straight and get in line to make sure you
got into soccer? No, don't answer that, I want you

to think—really think—about why it's okay to call someone your parent because they insulted us.

TEEJ He didn't.

FREDA Yes, he did, and so did you.

TEEJ I'm sorry.

FREDA Think about it, Teejay.

TEEJ Mom—I'm sorry, I didn't think—

FREDA You have two parents.

TEEJ I—want a dad.

FREDA Teejay, I understand. You're a boy; you're surrounded by women—I get it. It must feel like hell sometimes.

TEEJ It doesn't, that's not it—

FREDA But Steven can't solve that. He can be someone you talk to. Or nod with. But just remember one thing about Steven—he is *not* your father.

TEEJ You don't have to hate me for this. I said I was *sorry*.

FREDA Fine.

TEEJ Fine. See what I mean? You don't understand *anything*. Nobody does. I'm going to Brian's.

He leaves.

FREDA   *(to the door)* Don't you leave, Teejay—*do not* leave!

SCENE 14.

JEM   My dad had a temper too. For no good reason he would just lose it on us. If we ever spilled anything at the supper table, that would be it, my dad's fist would come down—*bam*—he'd scream "*What. Did. You. Do*??!!" and my little sister would run out of the room terrified, which would just piss him right off, and he'd march after her and bring her back to the table and she'd be wailing and gasping and shaking and my mother would serve out the canned vegetables. I'd just be glaring at that bastard. I'd be thinking, "You don't even know how lucky you are. If I had what you had, man, I would never throw it away." I thought I would know, from watching him, how to hold on to what really mattered.

SCENE 15.

Flashback.

FREDA   Come on. We have to.

JEM   I don't want to.

FREDA   But Myrna said.

JEM   Still.

FREDA   Come on. I hate it when you . . .

JEM   No.

FREDA   Don't you want to fix us?

JEM   We're not broken.

FREDA   We are. A little. Come on—try. Please, Jem. We
need it.

JEM   We need . . . something, but not this. We need . . . space.

FREDA   No, we need intimacy. We need connection. We need to do this. Myrna said. Now come on . . . do it with me—I hate it when you . . .

JEM   I hate it when you tell me what we *need,* like what you're doing right *now.*

FREDA   Great! Okay, I hate it when you drink the orange juice out of the carton.

JEM   I hate it when you talk in a soft voice when you're mad.

FREDA   I hate it when you yell.

JEM   I hate it when you ask me if I think you're fat.

FREDA   I hate it when you brush your teeth outside of the bathroom—especially in the living room and it gets on the couch.

JEM   I do not.

FREDA   Hey, you're breaking the rules—you're not allowed to argue with my "hates." I get an extra one then. I hate it when you don't think you're the kids' real mother.

JEM   I hate it when you get preachy, like right now.

FREDA   I hate it when you are defensive.

JEM   I hate it when you pretend being a grad student is as hard as being a plumber.

FREDA   Ouch! Okay, okay—I hate it when you barge into the house and you tell me all about your day and never ask me about mine.

JEM   I'm working on that.

FREDA   Not allowed—I get an extra hate then. I hate it when you get so defensive and interrupt me and it's all about you—

JEM   You already said you hated that—you double hated the same thing.

FREDA   That's because I double hate your defensiveness. What do you double hate?

JEM   That's not how Myrna said to do it.

FREDA   Do it—double hate something.

JEM   You.

FREDA   What?

JEM   You! I hate you, Freda, and I double hate you, okay? Are you happy now? Your little game worked. I hate you!

FREDA   You're serious.

JEM   I have never been more serious in my life. I hate
you. I hate living with you. I hate how you're always
right. I hate how you're always telling me what to
do. I hate how you put me down.

FREDA   When did I—?

JEM   Hey! What about the rules? Do *I* get an extra hate
now?? Are you happy now, Freda? We're playing
your stupid little game, and guess what? We *hate each
other.*

SCENE 16.

Present. Outside.

SAM   Under our old tree-house tree, eh, buddy?

TEEJ   Hey, I'm not your buddy—quit calling me that—

SAM   Remember the time Jem made us all pickle-and-cheese sandwiches out here but she forgot hers inside?

TEEJ   We thought she was coming right back and we waited and waited.

SAM   And then I caught you sneaking a bite—you were such a *cute* little kid.

TEEJ   I'm not cute.

SAM   Yes you are—you are still *cute*.

TEEJ   I'm not—*quit* calling me that.

SAM   Okay, what's with you—

TEEJ   *I mean it.* You think you can call me anything you want—buddy, cute, little man—I'm sick of it.

SAM   Thanks for being mad at Jem and taking it out on me, eh.

TEEJ   I'm not mad at her.

SAM   Those are all the names *she* calls you—not me—

TEEJ   They're not—

SAM   Fine. Why are you in denial anyways?

TEEJ   Why are you?

SAM   How am I in denial? Wasn't it obvious to you? They can hardly even be in the same room without going off on each other—open your eyes, Bud.

TEEJ   *Quit calling me that—I mean it.*

SAM   Whoa, Teejay.

TEEJ   Say you're sorry.

SAM   Teejay—stop it.

TEEJ   Say it.

SAM   What is with you, Teejay?

TEEJ   *SAY IT!!!*

SAM   Okay, okay—I'm sorry, okay? I'm sorry.

            Long silence.

            I mean it. I am. I get it, you're getting older. I forget
            sometimes, okay? Okay?

            Long silence.

            Look, let's not be mad at each other—let's be mad
            at *them.*

TEEJ   Yeah.

SAM   They just shouldn't have had kids. You know? You
            don't go and make a big deal of having kids, going
            out and finding the sperm and everything—

TEEJ   What about my *Adventure Time* posters? I can't split
            them up—they're a set. And all my *Hunger Games*
            books—I want them all in one place. How do I keep
            them beside my bed if my bed keeps changing?

SAM   Our parents are assholes.

TEEJ   Why are they doing this? I don't want to move out.

SAM   Me neither.

TEEJ   Yeah.

SAM	Hey, Teej?
TEEJ	Yeah?
SAM	I'm really scared, you know? I mean, I know I'm always going off about them, but they *are* our moms, you know? From when we were little. From forever.
TEEJ	Yeah.
SAM	I'm going to miss us. What about all the food that Jem makes—
TEEJ	What about her corny jokes?
SAM	I know, eh? She always has to repeat it like ten times to milk the laugh.
TEEJ	And what about when she says, "Come on, everybody, let's have a family moment"?
SAM	Yeah, how are we supposed to have a family moment when we don't even have a family?
TEEJ	Why are they splitting up, anyways?
SAM	Freda's having an affair.
TEEJ	No she isn't.
SAM	She is and we're so screwed. Our family is over.
TEEJ	Wait, what's an affair mean exactly?

SAM   Another girlfriend.

TEEJ   You mean she's *cheating*? She wouldn't cheat on us.
            It's not true—

SAM   I'm telling you it's true.

TEEJ   How could she cheat on us? When would she do it?

SAM   I don't know, at night maybe. When she says she's
            going out for school, or to meetings. I don't know,
            I'm trying not to think about it—it makes me
            feel sick—

TEEJ   Our family's over.

FREDA   *I asked her to kiss me.* Claire. I've known her forever. Funny, she never quite took to Jem. I just chalked it up to them being so different. Jem as straight-talking as they come, and her—past butch, fluid, more into words and ideas . . . I am at her house, like I normally am, after our Queers Against Censorship meeting. She's making me tea, chatting away about the meeting, and she can tell I am upset. "What is it?" she says. "Nothing, I'm fine." But she pushes back—she wants to know—so I tell her. "I'm not happy." She brings me the tea and she is watching me. Something about the way she is watching me—like it matters whether the tea is good, whether it is too hot, the right flavour—it gets me, her look. I can't even look back, and it was the opposite of how Jem would be with me—"Why aren't you drinking the tea? What'd I do? How did I mess up now?"—and it's not even about Jem— it's about me. I want to feel good loving someone. I feel good when I'm with her. "Kiss me. Kiss me here at your table." Claire kisses me at her kitchen table with all my clothes on and I feel naked and starving, sweet tea running down my legs, her warm kisses covering me like the best conversation, and so I start laughing—that deep belly laugh like an explosion.

SCENE 18.

Flashback. FREDA *and* JEM *are drinking champagne.*

FREDA   Okay, okay—repeat after me—I promise.

JEM   I promise.

FREDA   I, Jem.

JEM   I, Jem.

FREDA   Do take this Freda.

JEM   Do take this Freda.

FREDA   To have and to hold.

JEM   To have and to hold.

FREDA   In sickness and in health.

JEM	In sickness and in health.
FREDA	For all our babies.
JEM	What?
FREDA	Say it, say it—for all our babies.
JEM	What—
FREDA	Come on.
JEM	For all our—?
FREDA	Yes.
JEM	Really?
FREDA	Yes.
JEM	You want to—
FREDA	I do.
JEM	With me—?
FREDA	With you. Because you—we—are going to be beautiful parents. We're going to make sweet, adorable little babies. We're going to love them to the moon and you're going to tell them funny stories and make them laugh and hold them when they're sick.

JEM I'll teach them the difference between a ratchet and a wrench.

FREDA You'll be great.

JEM We will love them to the moon.

FREDA To the moon.

SCENE 19.

*Present. JEM and FREDA in the kitchen.
They are looking at TEEJAY's report card.*

JEM   That little asshole. That little bastard—forty-nine
absences and failing every subject. Where the *fuck*
was he? I'll fucking kill that kid—

FREDA   Can we just wait—before you go apeshit—can we
wait and hear his side of the story—?

JEM   Right, your precious little baby, let him walk all
over you—

FREDA   Jem, stop it. I can't stand the way you talk
about him.

JEM   Go ahead, make excuses for him—he's in trouble,
Freda.

FREDA   *I know* that, Jem, but this is us—*we* did this to him.
He's upset—about us—and maybe if he's not

showing up at school, maybe there's a good reason. Did you ever think about that? Maybe he's being threatened—maybe he's scared—and we haven't even noticed. We've been so caught up in our own shit.

JEM   Come on, get over yourself, Freda, and quit making excuses. He's in trouble—he's skipping school—his fault, not ours. You can't just let him off the hook here, okay?

FREDA   *Teejay*—get up here.

        SAM enters.

SAM   What's happening?

JEM   Teejay has forty-nine absences and failed *every* subject. And, oh yeah, Freda wants to think that this is our fault—

FREDA   Jem, why are you doing this?

SAM   You mean he failed everything and you *just* noticed—*great parenting!*

        TEEJAY enters.

TEEJ   What the hell—

FREDA   Teejay, where were you—

        She thrusts the report card in his face.

And what's going on, Teejay? Look at this!

TEEJ What?

FREDA Forty-nine absences. Where do you go when you leave here in the morning, Teejay!?

TEEJ To school—

JEM Don't lie to us—where do you go? Where. Do. You. Go.

TEEJ Forget it. I can't explain anything to you—you don't get it.

FREDA I don't care what you think I get or do not get, Teejay—you are going to tell me. Forty-nine absences, failing *every* subject. Did you think we would never find out—?

TEEJ Please. Don't break up.

JEM *Don't change the subject, Teejay—where do you go?*

FREDA *Jem*! Let me deal with this, okay?

JEM *We* are dealing with Teejay!

FREDA Where do you go, Teejay? Tell us *now*.

TEEJ Don't yell at me.

FREDA Jem, give us a minute here—

TEEJ   *No.*

SAM   Leave my brother alone!

TEEJ   I just don't want you to go, okay—

JEM   Hey, buddy, it's going to be all right—okay? We're going to get through this. Now tell us, Teejay—please—where do you go when you don't go to school—?

TEEJ   What's the big deal? I just go to Brian's. Nobody's home there—

JEM   Video games—it's like a poison.

TEEJ   It's quiet. Nobody talks to us, nobody yells, just the sound of guns going off on our guys. And we fight back. We're unbeatable now—we're at the highest level now all the time. Our guys—we control them—they're not afraid of anything, they own the streets. The other day Brian's guy killed a gang of forty—coolest thing ever. He just stood there like he wasn't afraid at all—shooting and shooting and shooting—killed all the bad guys dead.

SCENE 20.

JEM   I never counted on kids. I didn't think that was ever going to be something that I would get to do. I knew I'd never get pregnant, but I didn't think I was going to ever even *know* anyone pregnant, let alone be lovers with them. No, sir, you came out into the bar scene in Montreal and you drank your beer and you had your job and you had a girlfriend if you were lucky—and the bar scene, it was hard core—the drinks cost twice as much and the liquor was only half as strong. The doors were locked with chains and you had to let the guard dogs sniff you to get in.

The lights were red mostly, but if they ever turned white, that meant the cops were raiding the place and you had to hightail it out of there as fast as you could. We never talked about kids back then—kids would ruin everything. Kids would be like what's the point of being a dyke if you're just going to do that—no, we were living outside of the mould. We were revolutionaries. Where were kids going to fit in all of that? No, you gave up that notion and there was a point where you thought about it and it was kind of a relief, you know—no little noses to worry about, no teeth to put braces on, nobody to mess up your date night, nobody extra to fall in love with who could make you feel like you would have to die if you ever lost them—

SCENE 21.

Flashback. The morning after their first
night. JEM walks in with tea.

JEM   I just want to lay here and watch you. It's kind of a dream, you know, someone like you—

FREDA   Come on, you probably have someone new in your bed all the time.

JEM   No—been travelling solo for quite a while actually.

FREDA   Not last night.

JEM   True—

JEM grabs FREDA playfully.

I've got you now!

FREDA   What? Hey! Okay, okay, you win, you win.

JEM	Say it—come on— You are the strongest.
FREDA	*(trying to get free)* Ahh—you are the strongest.
JEM	You are the strongest, Uncle Jem.
FREDA	You are the strongest, Uncle Jem.
JEM	And I am so glad I came home with you last night.
FREDA	And I am so glad I came home with you last night.
JEM	Nice—that's what I like to hear.

She releases FREDA. *They lie together out of breath.* FREDA *jumps* JEM.

FREDA	Now I've got you.
JEM	Yeah, you do—what are you going to do with me?
FREDA	I don't know. What should I do with someone who held me down and forced me to say all kinds of things?
JEM	Maybe you should make me say things too.
FREDA	All right—how about Freda is fun.
JEM	Freda is fun.
FREDA	And beautiful.

JEM   And beautiful.

FREDA   And butchier than me.

JEM   What? Would you lay off that—*ow*—what—

FREDA   And butchier than me.

JEM   No.

FREDA   Oooh, you're serious. Ooh, I have touched something there, haven't I? You don't want me messing with your butchiness.

JEM   It's me—it's mine. Being a butch—saved my life.

SCENE 22.

JEM   It wasn't easy being a little baby butch in the sub-urbs. The kids started saying I had tendencies. I hated that. Tendencies. They used the other word too in front of that. Lesbian. Lesbian. Tendencies. Those two words. I mean each of them on their own is bad enough, but together. Lesbian. Sounds like Martian. Or alien. Or some creature—when I was sixteen I got a car and drove downtown. There was this bar—the Virgina—dark, smoky, full of women. The bathroom had these kind of saloon swinging doors—like what is that with the lesbian Western motif—anyways, I went inside and there was this old grey-haired butch grinning away at me—like she was seeing herself in me all over again. So what if I was too young to drink? She bought me beers that I drank with a straw, that big old grinning butch. We never even talked—just sat there—and I let her put her hand on my knee. At first it was okay. I told myself I could just let her do that—what was the harm? But after a while her hand on my knee weighed a hundred pounds and her breath smelled rotten every time she let out a laugh. Her little whispy moustache needed a trim badly and I thought, "Is this going to be my life?" This hole in the wall that reeked of yesterday's bleach and an old crate of pickled eggs, the vinegar sticking in my throat all through my drive home—speeding down the Décarie Expressway with the windows wide open and the night air rushing at my ears. "I'm in it too deep," I thought. "I'll never get out."

I'd get home from that bar, close my bedroom door and take way too many Aspirins, shut my eyes, and wait for the dreams to come.

SCENE 23.

Flashback. JEM*'s braiding* SAM*'s hair.*

JEM   Your hair is so fly-away, that's the trouble—like
       Freda's—her hair is hard to braid too—

SAM   Well?

JEM   What?

SAM   Aren't you going to do the song?

JEM   What—that? From when you were so little? Okay, so,
       I take the hair and I divide it into three piles—one
       for Dorothy the elephant—

       She pulls a bit of hair away.

—one for Rose the mouse—

       She pulls another bit of hair away.

—and one for the time that they both shared a house.

She pulls each bit in turn.

BOTH Uh-oh *(pulls)*—uh-oh *(pulls)*—uh-oh *(pulls)*.

JEM There—let's see the handiwork. *(examining)* Pretty good.

SAM Hey, Mom?

JEM Yeah?

SAM Can I have twenty bucks, Mom?

JEM Why?

SAM I can pay you back next week. Thanks, Momma—

JEM Wait. You've gotta tell me what it's for, sweetheart.

SAM Stuff—

JEM What kind of stuff?

SAM I don't know—personal *stuff.* Why do you need to know?

JEM If you want my money, you gotta tell me what it's for.

SAM	Why? Why do you treat me like I'm a *child?* I'm not—fine. Forget it, I don't need your stinky plumber money anyways—
JEM	Hey, don't talk to me like that.

FREDA enters.

FREDA	What's going on?
SAM	Ask her—she needs to know everything. I asked if I could borrow some money. What's the big deal? I'm just going out. With Perry.
FREDA	Who's Perry?
JEM	*No way! You don't even know this guy—*
FREDA	Jem, it's okay, give her a minute. Let's all calm down. Sam, explain, honey, tell us, who is this guy?
SAM	It doesn't matter anyways—it's not like any of them ever stick around.
JEM	What's that supposed to mean?
SAM	Once they find out about my "*dyke*" moms. One of them is pretty and one of them is—whatever—they either get super grossed out, or they want to know everything, like what do I call you, or what are you like with each other. And then they basically all say the stupidest things so I have to dump them before they dump me—don't know why it's so hard

to understand. Doesn't everyone have a mother who wants to get a special card on the third Sunday in June?

JEM   You don't say that.

FREDA   That was one year and then we stopped.

SAM   Daddy-o Day? Come on—that went on for years.

JEM   *Quit being so rude.* And let me tell you something, miss—you are not going anywhere with this guy Perry!

SAM   Why?

JEM   *Because I said so.*

FREDA   Jem, sweetie, let's all take a minute here, okay? Sam's growing up. We have to start letting her do what she needs to do.

SAM   Yeah, time to cut the apron strings, Daddy-o—

JEM   *Don't call me that.*

SAM   *Why? You act just like a mean old Daddy-o—Daddy-o—* but oh, too bad you don't have any balls.

JEM   *(to SAM, as she exits) Fuck you!*

FREDA   Are you out of your mind?

JEM	Did you hear what she called me?
FREDA	What she called you? What about what you said to her?
JEM	She can handle it—she's got a trash mouth—
FREDA	I can't do this, Jem—
JEM	What are you talking about? Sam talks worse than that—
FREDA	I don't even know you anymore—
JEM	Why are you going there, Freda? You want to pit me against the kids, fine. You know what? You are living in a dream bubble—oh, let's have kids, and you're going to be a great mother—*yeah right*! I can't get anywhere near those kids and you know it and they know it. Why don't you just take your precious little kids and see how well you do without me.
FREDA	I will do fine without you.
JEM	What's that supposed to mean?
FREDA	You just told me take my precious little kids and leave you—
JEM	I didn't say that—I said you *can't* leave me.
FREDA	You did—you said, "Take your precious little kids and see how well you do without me."

JEM	Okay, so I said it—I didn't mean it like *that*.
FREDA	Right.
JEM	I'm sorry. I didn't mean it like that. You know that.
FREDA	It doesn't work like that.
JEM	I'm *sorry. Come on—*
FREDA	No, Jem, you can't keep apologizing everything away, besides—
JEM	What—
FREDA	I don't love you anymore.
JEM	What?
FREDA	I stopped. Being in love with you.
JEM	Since when?
FREDA	I don't know. A while.
JEM	Are you in love with someone else?
FREDA	No. Nobody. Just not you.
JEM	Don't do this, Freda. We have kids. Come on. Twenty-one years.
FREDA	Don't—don't touch me, Jem.

JEM	You used to love it when I touched you. You used to say my touch was electric. I rearranged your cells.
FREDA	Your touch—ha, that's a joke—electric? When's the last time you kissed me, Jem?
JEM	I kissed you this morning.
FREDA	You kissed me goodbye—on the cheek.
JEM	So let me kiss you now.
FREDA	It doesn't work that way, Jem.
JEM	You've gone ice cold on me. Cold and—
FREDA	Call me names if you want.
JEM	I'm sorry.
FREDA	Don't, Jem—
	(JEM touches her) I don't feel anything. We are over. We are really over.
JEM	*(holding onto FREDA)* No—no no—no—
FREDA	Don't.
JEM	Please—please—please, Freda.
FREDA	No—no.

JEM	I'm sorry.
FREDA	You are *always* sorry. You're *sorry*—you're *sorry*—we don't need to fight anymore or hurt each other— we can have peace in our lives.
JEM	I don't want peace. I want you.
FREDA	I want peace. I don't want you.
JEM	I want you—I want *you*.

SCENE 24.

JEM   This truck pulls up beside us—it was early days—with this guy in there leering, like really creepy just staring at us. I drop Freda's hand but she doesn't want to. She looks up at me like, "Come on, it's okay—it's a free country." So we keep holding hands. The truck drives away and my heart's beating hard. Freda leans up on her tippy toes—she gives me the sweetest kiss as if to say, "See, we're allowed"—then we hear it, the truck backing up, its engine revving like a beast, the guy going, "That your girlfriend?" And I have the sense to say no, but Freda—she always had guts—she says, "Yeah, what if it is?" and the guy gets out of his truck—big, stocky muscular guy, ugly as shit—stands in our way, and says, "Why don't you show me how you do it." We turn around and run.

I hated that moment—running for our lives with him yelling after us, "Hey, get back here, you ugly dykes." I still wonder—should we have ran? Was I a coward? Am I a coward? Do you always stay and fight? Or, is it smart to know when to get the hell out?

SCENE 25.

Present. JEM *and the kids are moving out.* JEM *holds the candlesticks.*

JEM   Goodbye, Freda.

FREDA   Goodbye, Jem.

JEM   I don't hate you.

FREDA   I know. I don't hate you either.

JEM   This feels like shit.

FREDA   It'll be better tomorrow.

JEM   I guess. Hey, does everyone have it this hard or is it just us?

It's just us.

JEM gives FREDA *the candlesticks.*

I don't hate you.

FREDA   I know.

SCENE 26.

They exit, one at a time, except JEM. The exit should convey a feeling that the family is broken, but will find a way to carry on and stay together in a different form. The music from the opening scene is reprised. The stage is left with JEM looking back at the house.

Lois Fine has been widely published in
anthologies, newspapers, magazines,
and journals across various genres. Her
article "Outlaw Moms," first published in
NOW Magazine and later in the anthol-
ogy *Who's Your Daddy?*, documents her
and others' successful Ontario charter
challenge regarding queer parenting.
Lois lives in Toronto.

First edition: March 2016
Printed and bound in Canada by Imprimerie Gauvin, Gatineau

Cover photo of Kathryn Haggis by Tanja-Tiziana Burdi

**PLAYWRIGHTS
CANADA PRESS**

202-269 Richmond St. W.
Toronto, ON
M5V 1X1

416.703.0013
info@playwrightscanada.com
playwrightscanada.com

A **bundled** eBook edition is available
with the purchase of this print book.

CLEARLY PRINT YOUR NAME ABOVE IN UPPER CASE

Instructions to claim your eBook edition:
1. Download the BitLit app for Android or iOS
2. Write your name in **UPPER CASE** above
3. Use the BitLit app to submit a photo
4. Download your eBook to any device

MIX
Paper from
responsible sources
FSC® C100212
www.fsc.org